Mexican Rule
of California

Heather Price-Wright

Consultants

Kristina Jovin, M.A.T.
Alvord Unified School District
Teacher of the Year

Vanessa Ann Gunther, Ph.D.
Department of History
Chapman University

Publishing Credits

Rachelle Cracchiolo, M.S.Ed., *Publisher*
Conni Medina, M.A.Ed., *Managing Editor*
Emily R. Smith, M.A.Ed., *Series Developer*
June Kikuchi, *Content Director*
Marc Pioch, M.A.Ed., and Susan Daddis, M.A.Ed., *Editors*
Courtney Roberson, *Senior Graphic Designer*

Image Credits: Cover and p.1 DeA Picture Library/G. Dagli Orti/Granger, NYC; pp.2–3 Mapa de los estados unidos de Méjico : según lo organizado y definido por las varias actas del Congreso de dicha república, y construido por las mejores autoridades [graphic], G4410 1848 .D5, Courtesy of The Bancroft Library, University of California, Berkeley; pp.4, 11, 17, back cover North Wind Picture Archives; p.5 John Mitchell/Alamy Stock Photo; p.6 (bottom) Library of Congress [general.31218.1]; p.7 DeA Picture Library/G. Dagli Orti/Granger, NYC; pp.8–9, 29 (bottom) [View taken near Monterey, California], Robert B. Honeyman, Jr. collection of early Californian and Western American pictorial material [graphic], BANC PIC 1963.002:1306--FR. Courtesy of The Bancroft Library, University of California, Berkeley; p.10 Creative Commons Attribution-Share Alike 4.0 International by Shruti Mukhtyar; pp.12–13, 18, 26–27 Courtesy of the California History Room, California State Library, Sacramento, California; p.14 National Archives and Records Administration [595794]; p.15 The Protected Art Archive/Alamy Stock Photo; p.16 Classic Image/Alamy Stock Photo; p.17 (top) Photo by John Burgess/The Press Democrat; p.19 (top) Lebrecht Music and Arts Photo Library/Alamy Stock Photo, (full page) The life of a trapper: a sudden halt, Robert B. Honeyman, Jr. collection of early Californian and Western American pictorial material [graphic], BANC PIC 1963.002:1448--FR. Courtesy of The Bancroft Library, University of California, Berkeley; pp.20–21 Library of Congress [LC-DIG-ppmsca-09855]; pp.22–23 Granger, NYC; pp.24–25 Library of Congress [LC-DIG-highsm-20857]; p.25 (bottom) H.S. Photos/Alamy Stock Photo; p.26 (bottom) Nicholas Philip Trist Papers, 1795-1873, Manuscript Division, Library of Congress; p.28 Disefio de Los Alamos y Agua Caliente : [Calif.]/ [por Esteban Ardisson], U.S. District Court. California, Southern District. Land case 183 SD, page 86, Land Case Map D-1202. Courtesy of The Bancroft Library, University of California, Berkeley; p.29 (top) Native Californians lassoing a steer, Robert B. Honeyman, Jr. collection of early Californian and Western American pictorial material [graphic], BANC PIC 1963.002.1350-FR. Courtesy of The Bancroft Library, University of California, Berkeley, (middle) A California magnate in his home, The mission era [graphic]: California under Spain and Mexico and reminiscences, BANC PIC 19xx.039:33-FR. Courtesy of The Bancroft Library, University of Califomia, Berkeley; p.32 Library of Congress [LC-DIG-ppmsca-09855]; all other images from iStock and/or Shutterstock.

Library of Congress Cataloging-in-Publication Data

Names: Nussbaum, Ben, 1975- author.
Title: California's Indian nations / Ben Nussbaum.
Description: Huntington Beach, CA : Teacher Created Materials, [2017] | Includes index. | Audience: Grades 4-6.
Identifiers: LCCN 2017014089 (print) | LCCN 2017014329 (ebook) | ISBN 9781425835026 (eBook) | ISBN 9781425832322 (pbk.)
Subjects: LCSH: Indians of North America--California--Juvenile literature. | Gabrielino Indians--Juvenile literature. | Yokuts Indians--Juvenile literature. | CYAC: Yana Indians--Juvenile literature.
Classification: LCC E78.C15 (ebook) | LCC E78.C15 N87 2017 (print) | DDC 979.4/00497--dc23
LC record available at https://lccn.loc.gov/2017014089

Teacher Created Materials

5301 Oceanus Drive
Huntington Beach, CA 92649-1030
http://www.tcmpub.com

ISBN 978-1-4258-3236-0

© 2018 Teacher Created Materials, Inc.
Printed in China
Nordica.012019.CA21801581

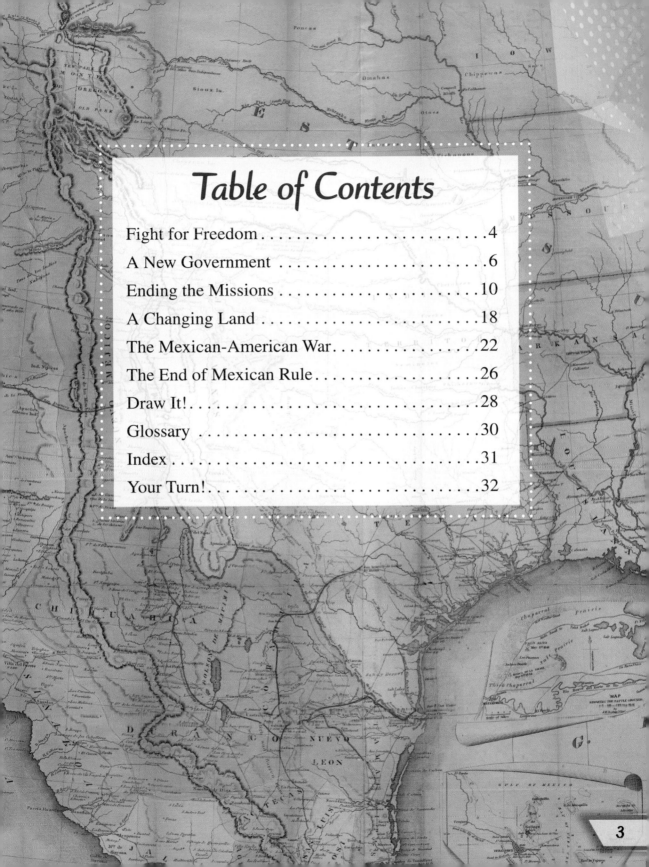

Table of Contents

Fight for Freedom

In 1810, a priest started Mexico's fight for freedom. Miguel Hidalgo y Costilla (hee-DALL-goh ee koh-STEE-yah) called for a revolt against Spain. He spoke at his church in the town of Dolores. His speech was called the *Grito de Dolores*, (GREE-toh deh deh-LOHR-ehs) or "Cry of Dolores." Costilla said, "My children…Will you free yourselves? Will you recover the lands stolen 300 years ago … by the hated Spaniards? We must act at once." His **congregation** was made up of American Indians and *mestizos*, or people of mixed races. They took his words to heart. They began the fight for freedom. Soon, others joined the fight.

The war against Spain lasted 11 years. In 1821, Mexico won the war. A new government came to power. People all over Mexico saw this as a new start. **Alta California** was now part of Mexico. The people there could start over, too.

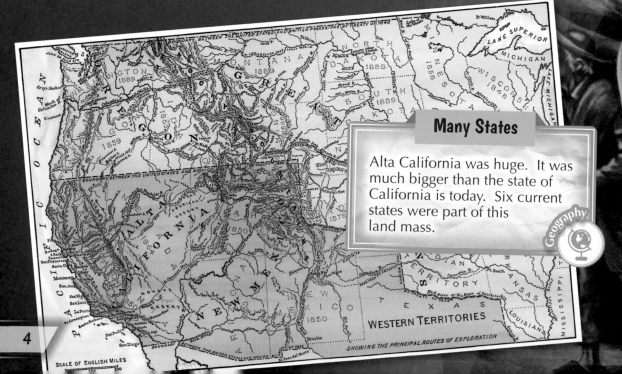

Many States

Alta California was huge. It was much bigger than the state of California is today. Six current states were part of this land mass.

Costilla gives the *Grito de Dolores*.

Before the Grito

Costilla was born into a large family. He was the second child born out of 11. To become a priest, he attended San Nicolás Obispo. When his older brother died, he became the head priest of the local church. As he got older, he became concerned with how the Spanish rulers were treating the Mexican people.

A New Government

The new Mexican government had a lot of work to do. Its leaders had to decide how to rule. One of the first steps was to set up laws. They wrote a new constitution. Then, they needed people to enforce the laws. They gave this power to Luis Antonio Argüello (ahr-GWEH-yoh). He was the first governor of Alta California under Mexican rule. He established a **council** to help him lead. But the council did not have much power. Rich Californios had power because they controlled most of the land. They were from Spanish families and spoke Spanish.

Argüello was in office for four years. One of his goals was to keep people safe. The soldiers in Alta California had not been paid for many years under Spanish rule. Argüello tried to collect taxes from the people to pay the soldiers.

In 1824, a new law passed. Mexican citizens could apply for **land grants** in the area. This was a huge change. It brought many people to the region.

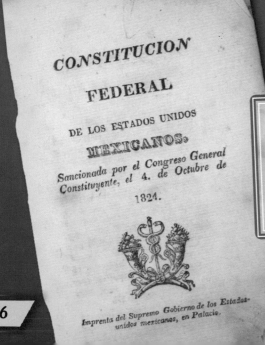

Constitutional Changes

In 1824, the first constitution was replaced with a new one. It included *Siete Leyes*, or "seven laws." These laws changed the structure of Mexico's government.

Civics

Governors

The early government of Mexico was not stable. There were many changes in leadership. This was true of Alta California, too. There were 16 Mexican governors in 24 years. Pío Pico was governor twice. The first time, he was in office for only 20 days. Later, he would be the last governor before the United States would take this land.

Civics

Mexico celebrates its independence.

Clashes with Locals

The new leaders made many promises to the American Indians. Under Spanish rule, many native people were forced to live at the missions. They went to schools and worked there, too.

Under Mexican rule, they were made citizens. They were granted some rights. They could vote and own land. They could even run for office. But in reality, they were not treated fairly. In the first 10 years of Mexican rule, hundreds of land grants were given. Only 51 of those went to native people.

Mariano's Life

Mariano Vallejo (vah-YAY-hoh) was a key Californio. He was born when Mexico was still ruled by Spain. When he grew up, he became an important military leader. He helped found the town of Sonoma. The state named a city after him.

Some Californios settled near Monterey.

Most of the land was quickly taken from the American Indians. Some Californios married native women and claimed their land. Then they forced American Indians to stay and work on the land for unfair wages. Some native people fought back. They **raided** Mexican farms. They opposed their poor treatment.

In 1825, a new Mexican governor was chosen. His name was José María de Echeandía (deh eh-chehn-DEE-ah). He let American Indians who had lived at the missions for at least 10 years claim and work on their own pieces of land. But they were not really free. As part of the new rule, they had to give parts of their earnings from their lands to the government.

Joining Forces

During Mexican rule, many American Indians moved inland. They joined tribes there. Some of the inland tribes included native people who had run away from the missions before. Banding together, they raided farms. They stole **livestock**, mostly horses. They used the horses for food or sold them.

Ending the Missions

The missions were a big part of Alta California under Spanish rule. The priests in charge were powerful. They controlled life at the missions for everyone. The Mexican leaders wanted to change this. They secularized the missions. That meant the church was no longer in control of the land. The mission system ended in 1833.

Mission Lands

Each mission was built on valuable land. The Mexican leaders had to make some decisions. The land would be divided, with some of it going to native people who lived at the missions. The rest of the land and buildings would be turned over to the local towns. Officials there would decide how to use them.

Californios wanted to take control of the land. They knew money was needed to rule this region. The mission lands could help. The plan was to use the land to produce income for Mexico.

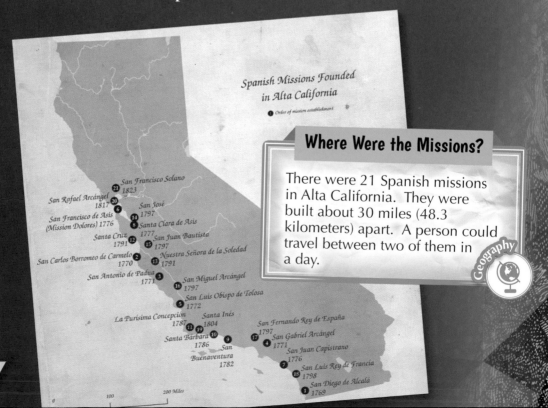

Spanish Missions Founded in Alta California

● Order of mission establishment

San Francisco Solano
21 1823
San Rafael Arcángel 20
1817
San José
San Francisco de Asis 6 14 1797
(Mission Dolores) 1776 8 Santa Clara de Asis
Santa Cruz 12 1777 San Juan Bautista
1791 15 1797
San Carlos Borromeo de Carmelo 2 13 Nuestra Señora de la Soledad
1770 1791
San Antonio de Padua 3
1771 16 San Miguel Arcángel
1797
5 San Luis Obispo de Tolosa
1772
La Purísima Concepción Santa Inés
1787 11 19 1804
Santa Bárbara 10 San Fernando Rey de España
1786 San 1797 San Gabriel Arcángel
Buenaventura 4 1771
1782 San Juan Capistrano
1776
7 San Luis Rey de Francia
18 1798
San Diego de Alcalá
1 1769

0   100   200 Miles

Where Were the Missions?

There were 21 Spanish missions in Alta California. They were built about 30 miles (48.3 kilometers) apart. A person could travel between two of them in a day.

Geography

The Missions' Purpose

The Spanish wanted to "civilize" American Indians. They taught the native people about the Catholic faith. They forced the native people to work at the missions.

A missionary speaks to a group of California Indians.

Land for American Indians

The mission lands were divided. Half of each mission became **communal** property. This land was made into town **plots** for farming. American Indians were promised some of this land. The rest of the mission land was given away. This was done through land grants.

Many native people received mission lands. But they did not know what a land grant was. They were not aware that they owned the land. Some even walked away from their land. They just wanted to leave the missions.

Californios wanted the land. Many times they were able to trick native people into selling their land. Sometimes, California Indians were forced to sell their land. They were not paid fair prices.

Hardships for Indians

Many of the American Indians were from inland areas. After the mission system ended, they returned to their homelands. But, starting over would be very hard. Native people's diets had been made up of plants before. During the mission years, tribal lands had been turned into grazing areas. The animals had ruined the plant life. The American Indians' food source was gone.

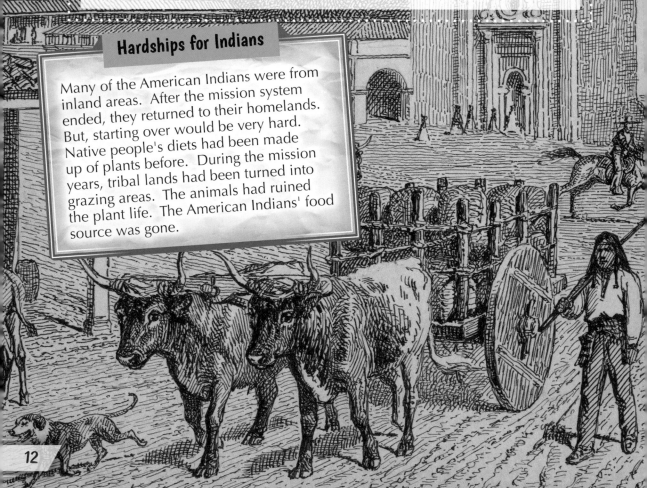

Native Life Today

Today, there are more than 100 tribes in California. They vary in size. Some tribes have as few as five members, while the biggest tribes have close to 5,000. Tribes are found all over the state, in rural and urban areas.

Mission San Luis Rey

Mission Land Grants

Mexican leaders gave out more than 500 land grants. People were excited at the chance to get land for free. The leaders wanted people to use the land to raise cattle and to farm. This would help the region's economy grow.

In order to receive a land grant, a person had to make a map of the area they were asking for. These were hand-drawn maps called *diseños* (dih-SEHN-yohs). They showed important landmarks, such as rivers and hills.

Californios received much of the mission lands through land grants. They set up ranchos and raised livestock. Most ranchos were located in what is now Southern California. This time is known as the *golden age of the rancho period*. It lasted for 13 years.

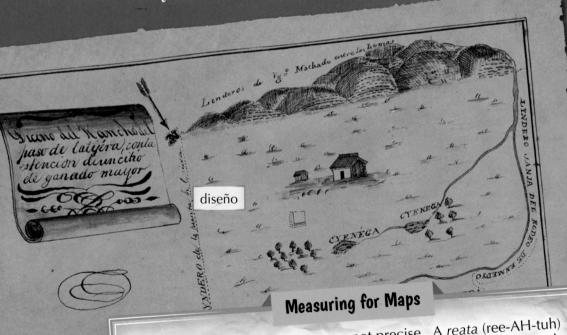

diseño

Measuring for Maps

Measuring tools at that time were not precise. A *reata* (ree-AH-tuh) was a tool used to measure large areas. This was a rope with a pole tied to each end. One rancher would hold a pole while another walked until the *reata* was pulled as far as it could reach. They repeated these steps until the whole area was measured.

THE OLD
SPANISH AND MEXICAN
RANCHOS
OF LOS ANGELES COUNTY

Land Grant Rules

Land-grant holders had to meet certain requirements of the government. They had to promise to use the land for raising animals or growing crops. They had to build a home on the land within a year. They couldn't rent the land to others or block public roads.

Civics

The Rancho Period

Rancho owners mainly raised cattle. They ate or sold beef from their herds. They also sold the animals' **hides** and **tallow**. Many of these families grew rich. They thought they were in a higher class than those who did not own land. They only socialized with other rancho owners.

Within a few years, Californios owned most of Alta California. As they grew richer, they bought more and more land. Those in need, mainly the American Indians, suffered. Mexican leaders had tried to help the American Indians. But it did not work out that way. In the end, the Mexican system was not much fairer to the native people than the Spanish one.

People make soap from tallow in a factory.

Making Tallow

Tallow is made from animal fat. It is used to make soap and candles. People also used it to cook. It is made by chopping up fat cut from beef and cooking it for a long time over very low heat. This process is called *rendering*.

Branding Cattle

Under Mexican rule, all cattle and horses needed brands. Each rancho had its own mark to show to whom the animals belonged. An owner placed a hot branding iron with the mark on the left hip of their cattle and horses. If the animal was sold, the new owner placed his mark on the left shoulder.

A Changing Land

Mexico wanted more people to come to Alta California to live. The leaders tried to get Mexicans to come. But many of them did not want to move. They thought this region was a **backwater**. It was too far away.

Newcomers

However, other people chose to come to Alta California. They wanted the chance to own land and get rich. To own land, foreigners had to become Mexican citizens. They also had to become Catholic.

People came from the United States and Europe to get land. These newcomers helped the region's growing economy. Locals still owned most of the ranchos. But newcomers set up their own farms. They **thrived** in other trades, too. Many were fur trappers. They traded tallow and hides from animals. With all the new people coming, the culture of Alta California began to change.

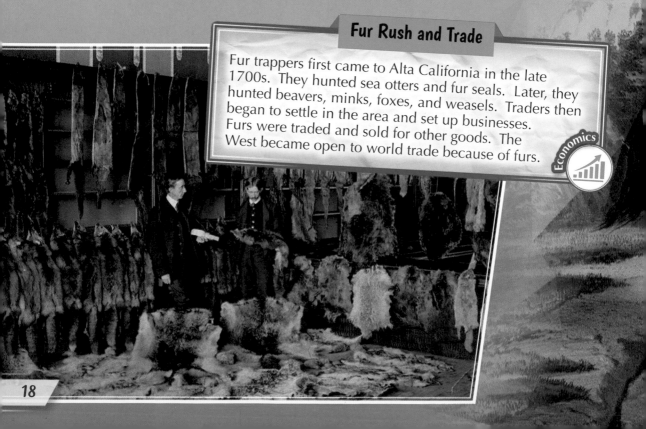

Fur Rush and Trade

Fur trappers first came to Alta California in the late 1700s. They hunted sea otters and fur seals. Later, they hunted beavers, minks, foxes, and weasels. Traders then began to settle in the area and set up businesses. Furs were traded and sold for other goods. The West became open to world trade because of furs.

Economics

Before the Mast

Two Years Before the Mast is a **memoir**. Richard Henry Dana Jr. wrote it. He was an American who sailed to Alta California. The book is about his trip and life at sea. He also writes about what California was like before the Gold Rush.

A group of fur trappers travel on horseback.

Many newcomers who moved to the region married into Californio families. John Gilroy was one example. He came from Scotland. He was the first English-speaking settler to become a Mexican citizen. Others soon followed. John Sutter came from Switzerland. He started Sutter's Fort. Later, gold would be found on his land. John Marsh came from Boston. He set up a colony in the Central Valley. Marsh was the first American doctor in the region. These new settlers brought their own cultures. They were more in touch with their home cultures than with Mexican culture.

Control of Alta California began to slip away from Mexico. The region had many natural resources that were unused. It had useful **ports** for trade. U.S. presidents since Andrew Jackson wanted the land. James K. Polk was ready to buy it. His chance would soon come.

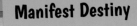

Manifest Destiny

The words *manifest destiny* were first used in 1845. The words came to mean that the United States was meant to stretch "from sea to shining sea." Many Americans thought that they had the right to expand and spread their ideas.

This famous painting symbolizes the United States expanding from coast to coast.

The Mexican-American War

The number of people in Alta California kept going up. By 1846, there were more than 1,000 Americans there. They helped to shape its culture. They played a big role in its trade and industries, too.

U.S. Interests

Settlers were not the only ones looking to come to California. The U.S. government was interested in it, too. The country had grown since its **founding**. Its leaders wanted more land and key ports. They thought this would help their young nation grow.

In 1835, U.S. President Andrew Jackson made an offer. He tried to buy the San Francisco Bay port. The port would help with trade. But Mexico said no. Ten years later, President James Polk tried to buy all of Alta California. Mexico said no again.

Mexico could not hold on to the land for much longer. There would be a fight for Alta California.

Border Disputes

One cause of the war between the United States and Mexico was a border dispute. They could not agree on what the Texas border should be between the two countries. The Americans wanted it to be the Rio Grande. Mexico wanted it to be the Nueces River.

Niños Héroes

In 1847, U.S. forces marched toward Mexico City. Their path was blocked by the Mexican military academy. The U.S. troops attacked. Most of the Mexican guards fled. A group of six young **cadets** stayed behind to defend the castle. They fought until their deaths. There is a monument in Mexico City to pay tribute to the *Niños Héroes*, or "Heroic Children."

The first battle of the Mexican-American War took place on May 8, 1846.

Mexican leaders did not have a strong hold over Alta California. They lived far away. Keeping track of all their land required more people and money than they had. In many areas, Mexicans and Americans fought over land.

Revolt

In 1846, José Castro caused a stir. He was a leader of the Mexican Army. He said land owned by foreign-born people would be taken back. The people who lived on these lands would be forced to leave the country. A group of Americans fought back in June at Sutter's Fort. This revolt was known as the *Bear Flag Revolt*.

One month before the revolt, the United States declared war on Mexico. The two countries would fight for the next two years.

Men raise the flag after the Bear Flag Revolt.

John Frémont

John Frémont was an American army officer. He may have planted the seeds of revolt. A couple months before the Bear Flag Revolt, he was at Sutter's Fort. He told the men in the area to prepare to rebel against Mexico.

The End of Mexican Rule

The United States won the war in 1848. In fact, its army did not lose one battle. More U.S. soldiers died from disease than from being in combat. Mexico lost close to one-third of its land. The United States took control of Alta California. In return, it paid Mexico $15 million. This was part of the **treaty** both countries signed.

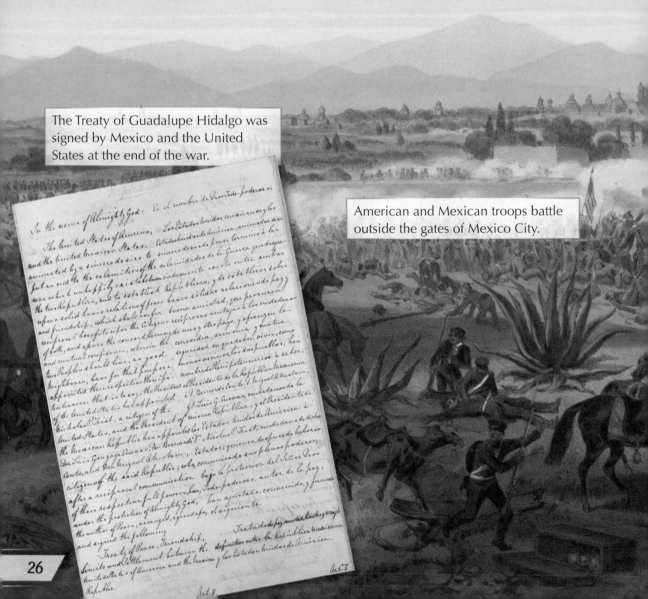

The Treaty of Guadalupe Hidalgo was signed by Mexico and the United States at the end of the war.

American and Mexican troops battle outside the gates of Mexico City.

Big changes were coming. The same year the war ended, gold was discovered at Sutter's Mill. California's population would grow by leaps and bounds. People from all around the world flocked to the territory. They hoped to get rich.

Mexican rule lasted just 27 years. However, Mexican **influences** can still be seen all around the state.

Hero of the War

Zachary Taylor was a hero in the Mexican-American War. He ran for president in 1848 and won. He died of an illness after being in office for less than two years.

Draw It!

Imagine you are applying for a land grant in California. The first requirement is to make a *diseño*. It should show what the land looks like, where it is, and how big the plot is.

- Think about your home and the land it is on. This is the land you are hoping to be granted.

- What is it shaped like? Draw an outline.

- How big is it? Californians at this time often didn't have official measurement tools. They improvised. How would you measure your land? Come up with a method. Note your measurements on your *diseño*.

- What is on your land? Think about natural features like trees, rocks, and water. Then, think about man-made items like houses, sheds, and barns. Add them to your drawing, and label them.

- What would you name your land? Come up with a creative name for your rancho.

Glossary

Alta California—land that was a colony of Spain and then Mexico; it included Nevada, Utah, and parts of California, Arizona, New Mexico, Wyoming, and Colorado

backwater—a quiet place, such as a small town, where there is not much progress or excitement

cadets—people who are training to be officers

communal—shared among everyone in a group or community

congregation—a gathering of people, usually for religious purposes

council—a group chosen to make rules, laws, or decisions

founding—the start of something; when something was established

hides—the skins of animals

influences—things that have the power to affect people or things

land grants—contracts that give ownership of plots of land

livestock—useful farm animals, such as cows, horses, and pigs, that are raised by people

memoir—a written account in which someone describes his or her past experiences

plots—areas of land that have been measured and designated for a particular purpose

ports—harbors where ships pick up and drop off goods

raided—attacked people or a place suddenly or unexpectedly

tallow—the fat from cows and sheep, which is used to make things like soap and candles

thrived—succeeded or prospered

treaty—a formal agreement made between two or more countries or groups

Index

Your Turn!

Symbolism

The 1872 painting above is titled *American Progress*. The artist used symbols to show progress in transportation and communication. It shows people moving west, first by covered wagon, then by stagecoach, and finally by train. The telegraph wire starts in the East (on the right) and allowed for faster communication with the West.

If you were to paint a modern picture of progress, what symbols would you use? Choose at least three examples of progress in transportation and communication. Then, explain why you chose them.